Cocurricular Activities:
Their Values and Benefits

Academic Societies and Competitions
Striving for Excellence

Career Preparation Clubs
Goal Oriented

Community Service
Lending a Hand

Foreign Language Clubs
Discovering Other Cultures

Hobby Clubs
Sharing Your Interests

Intramural Sports
Joining the Team

School Publications
Adventures in Media

Science and Technology Clubs
Ideas and Inventions

Student Government and Class Activities
Leaders of Tomorrow

Theater, Speech, and Dance
Expressing Your Talents

Vocal and Instrumental Groups
Making Music

Cocurricular Activities:
Their Values and Benefits

Student Government and Class Activities

Leaders of Tomorrow

Joann Vaars

Mason Crest Publishers

JUN 1 6 2005

Mason Crest Publishers, Inc.
370 Reed Road
Broomall, PA 19008
(866) MCP-BOOK (toll free)
www.masoncrest.com

First printing

1 2 3 4 5 6 7 8 9 10

Library of Congress Cataloging-in-Publication Data

Vaars, Joann.
   Student government and class activities: leaders of tomorrow/by Joann Vaars.
      p. cm.—(Cocurricular activities)
   ISBN 1-59084-898-5
   1. Student government. 2. Leadership—Study and teaching. I. Title. II. Series.
   LB3092.V25 2005
   371.5'9—dc22

      2004015864

Produced by
Choptank Syndicate, Inc. and Chestnut Productions, L.L.C.
260 Upper Moss Hill Road
Russell, Massachusetts 01071

Project Editors Norman Macht and Mary Hull
Design and Production Lisa Hochstein
Picture Research Mary Hull

OPPOSITE TITLE PAGE
A student government should reflect the diversity of the school's student body.

Table of Contents

Introduction

COCURRICULAR ACTIVITIES BUILD CHARACTER

Sharon L. Ransom
Chief Officer of the Office of Standards-Based Instruction
for Chicago Public Schools

Cocurricular activities provide an assortment of athletic, musical, cultural, dramatic, club, and service activities. They provide opportunities based on different talents and interests for students to find their niche while developing character. Character is who we really are. It's what we say and how we say it, what we think, what we value, and how we conduct ourselves in difficult situations. It is character that often determines our success in life and cocurricular activities play a significant role in the development of character in young men and women.

Cocurricular programs and activities provide opportunities to channel the interests and talents of students into positive efforts for the betterment of themselves and the community as a whole. Students who participate in cocurricular activities are often expected to follow certain rules and regulations that prepare them for challenges as well as opportunities later in life.

Many qualities that build character are often taught and nurtured through participation in cocurricular activities. A student learns to make commitments and stick with them through victories and losses as well as achievements and disappointments. They can also learn to build relationships and work collaboratively with others, set goals, and follow the principles and rules of the discipline, club, activity, or sport in which they participate.

Students who are active in cocurricular activities are often successful in school because the traits and behaviors they learn outside of the classroom are important in acquiring and maintaining their academic success. Students become committed to their studies and set academic goals that lead them to triumph. When they relate behaviors, such as following rules or directions or teaming with others, to the classroom, this can result in improved academic achievement.

Students who participate in cocurricular activities and acquire these character-rich behaviors and traits are not likely to be involved in negative behaviors. Peer pressure and negative influences are not as strong for these students, and they are not likely to be involved with drugs, alcohol, or tobacco use. They also attend school more regularly and are less likely to drop out of school.

Students involved in cocurricular activities often are coached or mentored by successful and ethical adults of good and strong character who serve as role models and assist students in setting their goals for the future. These students are also more likely to graduate from high school and go on to college because of their involvement in co-curricular activities.

In this series you will come to realize the many benefits of cocurricular activities. These activities bring success and benefits to individual students, the school, and the community.

Participating in student government is a great way to learn about civics. Many national political leaders got their start by becoming student council or class officers.

1

Functions of Student Government

No classroom can teach you more about civics and how representative government works than you can learn by becoming active in your school's student government. All students have the right to form a student body council and have a voice in school and district policies that affect them. But, like all rights, they are useful only when you choose to exercise them. If you sit on the sidelines and don't get involved in effecting changes in your school, using the rights and procedures afforded you, then you have less right to complain about things.

Assuming a position of leadership in your school can be your introduction to public service and working for the common good. There is much more to student government than just planning parties and having a good time. The student council represents the interests of the entire student body, from planning activities to working with the administration on policy issues.

The powers of a student government are spelled out

in a constitution. At most schools, this document allows students to have a voice in the policymaking decisions of administrators and school boards. That doesn't mean they have to do what the students demand; it just means your opinions and ideas will be heard. Your school's constitution can be amended to adjust to changing times and conditions in the school. Before getting involved in your student government, it's a good idea to read your constitution.

Student government, also known as the Associated Student Body (ASB), is usually headed by a president, vice-president, and secretary-treasurer, and includes class presidents and representatives, and a faculty advisor. Some of these offices may be elected and some appointed. Electing the top officers and allowing them to appoint other members of the council allows them to recruit members representing the variety of backgrounds and interests reflected in the makeup of the student body. In many schools, the more appointed officers and members the student council has, the more productive they are.

Constitutions vary as to how elections are held and the lengths of the terms of office. Some officers may be elected for a full school year; others' terms may be for only one semester. If you are interested in being a candidate for office or being appointed to the council, the ASB faculty advisor is the person who can provide you with guidance

Student Government Tip

Student leaders should meet regularly with the school's lead administrator to have their voices heard and to keep the school principal in touch with the students who are affected by administrative decisions.

All members of the student body should be encouraged to vote in student elections. Not all student government positions may be elective, though. Some schools also appoint students to serve in the student government.

on how to proceed. Some advisors hold workshops on elections and the functions of student government.

It's important to realize the visibility and responsibility that go with holding office. Student body representatives are held in high regard by their peers and teachers. Nothing can harm a student government more than its officers participating in questionable behavior.

Most schools have a leadership or student government class that elected and appointed council members must attend. This gives them a fixed time every day to work toward their goals. Some students think leadership class will be a snap, an "easy A." But grades for this class are based as much or more on how student leaders conduct the business of the council as on classroom work.

Exclusivity has no place in student government. There is no such thing as a student body officer "type." A variety of "types" is necessary in order to properly represent the many viewpoints on any campus. The student government should reflect the diversity of the student body. It's not easy to form a team from such a mixed group, but only by being widely representative can such a council gain the trust and credibility needed to be effective. Differences of opinion will occur within any governmental body. How they are reconciled and accommodated to form a consensus is a measure of the level of teamwork you've achieved.

The goal of student government is to make the school experience the best it can be for all the students. How to meet that goal is the challenge for each year's council. They may choose to focus on a specific issue and work to influence the policies dealing with it. They may come up with a theme for the year and direct all projects and activities toward that theme. These decisions must be made and reviewed regularly, as plans and events and circumstances change.

Not all decisions are easy. What is best for your school? When should you stand up for what you believe? How will your position or action affect the students you represent? These can be knotty problems and difficult decisions, unpopular among a large segment of the student population. But this comes with the territory. Governing is not always fun. There is more to student leadership than just feeling important walking around wearing a T-shirt or sweater with "ASB" on it.

Communicating with all of your constituents is of the utmost importance in running an effective and responsive

Identifying Student Leaders

"The key to the success of any student leadership group is to get good people who have a great work ethic, great attitude, and the time to commit," says Joe Fontana, Activities Director and leadership teacher at Menlo-Atherton High School in Atherton, California. "It takes a lot of hours. I spend a lot of time in late summer and early in the school year training them real well, then I'm able to step back. We eventually get to a democracy, but we pass through a dictatorship before we get there.

"How do you identify those good people? One way is through teachers. Halfway through the school year we talk to teachers and ask what kids would be good for leadership. I think a lot of student councils and leadership classes wind up with very outgoing, boisterous students who are really good at giving a speech, but that doesn't say anything about how well they will work or if they're able to start a project and finish it. The hardest part of any project is the middle. Everything looks like a failure in the middle, especially if you're planning something big.

"The only people who have to get up in front of a big group of people and give a speech are the ones who are running for student body office or class president. A lot of students are by nature very quiet. They couldn't do that. But when it comes to getting things done, they're as good as anybody. We seek them out, and that opens it up to a wider range of students. This is something I've learned over the years. You're going to have people who are loud, boisterous for rallies and that kind of thing. But mostly you need people who can get stuff done, are committed to the school, and have the time.

"At Menlo-Atherton, it isn't easy to get into a leadership class. We make students go through a lengthy process to qualify. They have to collect two hundred signatures, get a letter from a parent, one from a teacher, and one from a friend. They've got to take the time and energy. We make the process difficult, so it at least proves they can get something done."

At the Leaders Forum Core Camp, a camp for student leaders, campers share a little about who they are and where they come from.

student government. If you don't keep students, teachers, and administrators informed of what you are doing, you will fail before you begin. Homeroom representatives should be encouraged to attend council meetings and report back to their homerooms on activities and events being planned. Homeroom reps should also keep their teachers informed. While your faculty advisor can be a great help, requests for assistance will be better received and fulfilled if they come from fellow students than from teachers.

Working in secrecy doesn't work. Your school's daily bulletin should be used to publicize your actions. In addition to homeroom and bulletin information, utilize your school's bulletin boards and media outlets. This requires

Camps for Student Leaders

Many camps specialize in training student leaders. For more information, check out these Web sites:

www.nccj.org
The National Conference for Community and Justice (NCCJ), a human relations organization dedicated to fighting bias, bigotry, and racism in America, sponsors Camp Anytown, a residential youth program designed to break down stereotypes and bias and build respect and connections across group lines.

www.theleadersforum.com
The Leaders Forum Inc. trains high school students to take leadership initiative and build an environment for excellence. They offer a camp for student council or class officers that gives the student leaders a chance to meet with their peers from other schools and share ideas while learning leadership skills.

www.nhs.us/confprog
National Student Leadership Camps, sponsored by the National Association of Secondary School Principals (NASSP) are six-day experiential leadership programs for middle and high school student leaders and advisors that teach meeting management, goal setting, team building, project planning, conflict resolution, and service.

www.linkcrew.com
The Link Crew Freshman Transition Program, sponsored by Learning for Living, Inc., trains upperclassmen to help ease the transition to high school for incoming freshmen. Over four hundred thousand freshmen are welcomed to high school with Link Crew each year. The program uses fun activities, powerful messages, and genuine connections with others to help incoming ninth graders adjust to their new surroundings and learn what it takes to be successful in high school. The program lasts the entire year, beginning with an interactive freshman orientation and continuing with all kinds of academic and social follow-up activities.

Leadership Training

The Texas Association of Student Councils and Secondary School Principals has developed a student leadership course approved for elective credit. The course provides opportunities to study, practice, and develop group and individual leadership and organizational skills, including decision making, problem solving techniques, communications, leadership, human relations, and understanding the need for civic responsibility.

Students learn to apply these skills in dealing with peers, school administrators, and the community. The teacher's manual demonstrates an active, hands-on approach to leadership. The course is offered to all high school students in the state.

Topics included in the teacher's manual:

- Defining leadership

- The structure of leadership

- Meeting skills and parliamentary procedures

- Group dynamics and team building

- Problem solving

- Motivation

- Goal setting

- Communication

- Community/civic responsibility

- Additional resources

someone to coordinate getting the word out, keeping in mind the deadlines of the various media when necessary.

Getting people involved on campus may be one of the most difficult tasks student governments face in an era of apathy toward politics. Holding elections in a way that gives everyone a chance to be a candidate and to vote is crucial to making people feel that they have a voice in the

At the Leaders Forum Core Camp, students practice different student leadership scenarios. In this instance, they are discussing a potential crisis on campus.

system. Informing and connecting with uninvolved students and making them feel valued will redefine the climate on your campus. Making sure that a variety of groups on campus are represented on the student council gives everyone a reason to participate. There are many activities that disconnected students will become involved in if the right person asks them. Students who feel they are needed will respond.

High school is a time to spread your wings, to begin to form opinions and take leadership roles independent of parents and teachers. But that doesn't mean you have to choose between working with them and being independent. Parents like to be included, and teachers are there to help you because they like you. As one teacher commented, "If I just wanted to fill their heads with facts, I could teach on-line. The kids are why I show up and to not interact with them in a fun way would ruin my day."

Many parents' associations welcome the presence of

As a student leader, one of the most important things you can do is to reach out to your fellow students and inform them of what the student government is up to. Good communication is essential to a successful student government.

student council members at their meetings. They need to hear the students' viewpoint. They can also be a strong source of financial support for special projects and events. There may be specific tasks that you don't have the time or experience or resources to carry out. If parents are approached and asked to help in specific ways, they can be great partners. The same is true of your teachers. Working together, you can all help to make the school year a success. But remember, student government and student activities are basically of, by, and for the students. Parents and teachers are there to help, not to take over.

Being involved in student government will help you improve your school and the lives of your fellow students. It will also help you to gain valuable leadership experience as you represent the student body and participate in important school activities.

As a member of the student government, you will represent your fellow students to those in charge; help promote school spirit; show leadership by being a good communicator, problem solver, and a positive role model for others; promote awareness of important school issues; participate in fundraising activities, and possibly in community service projects as well.

You'll learn firsthand how government works and how to take leadership roles in other aspects of your life and career.

School climate activities should be designed to create an inclusive, positive school environment where all students feel they belong.

2

School Climate Activities

Every student government creates a school climate. This climate can be one of isolation, distrust, and dysfunction, or it can be a place where people feel engaged, appreciated, and valued. Students do not often realize that they are a larger part of the climate than teachers or administrators, and they can change a climate if they aren't happy with the way things are. After all, students outnumber staff. You do have power. Using the proper channels will work if your demands are reasonable.

When planning activities, it is important to remember that even an event designed for a specific purpose, such as a football game, black history month, or freshman bonding time, reaches out to everyone across the school. If students are told they are specifically not allowed or invited to participate, the message will resound in future activities. Even if something is planned grade specific, you can ask upper or lower classpeople to be involved through helping with music, food, or setting up, so everyone remembers that a school is a team. A grade specific dance is an activity that should not be considered. It's fine if the freshmen want to host a dance, but make sure that everyone is welcome to attend.

Everyone should feel special on their campus and be willing to stretch out of their comfort zone in a safe environment. Because we live in a world of global awareness, it is important to learn about and appreciate different ways of viewing the world. A first step toward embracing differences is to do so daily right on your own campus. Everyone on your campus should be treated with respect, even if they hold opinions that may differ from yours. Building empathy is one of the most important skills to learn in the twenty-first century.

There are also larger-scale things you can do on your campus. Since America is the "great salad bowl/melting pot," we know that everyone has an ethnicity that goes beyond being an American. Hosting a multicultural talent show is not just a fundraising opportunity; it is also a celebration of diversity and another chance to get your international students involved. Having students who can play the bagpipes, perform an Indian dance, drum a Native American ceremonial song, or perform rap, can make for a great show. You can top off the evening by offering or selling different ethnic foods (homemade ones are the best sellers).

If you are looking for some understanding of other groups, you may want to take students off campus to participate in some type of diversity training. One of the best in the country is Camp Anytown, run by the National Conference for Community and Justice (NCCJ). Formed more than forty years ago, this special camp has been featured on *The Oprah Winfrey Show* and is quite popular. It is

A great way to celebrate diversity on campus is to ask student body members from all different backgrounds to participate in a multicultural talent show.

worth working to persuade your school board to sponsor one or two students from your school to attend. Camp Anytown will ask for a specific demographic from your school and due to this, not everyone who wants to go will be accepted. Only about seventy-five students may attend each session. Many schools have a dual application process; teachers nominate specific students, and students may also apply by completing a self-nomination form.

At Camp Anytown, delegates learn about racism, sexism, and handicaps through exercises and talks. They discuss topics such as gender, class, ethnicity, and religion. The lessons they learn are taken home and shared. As one camper said, "Being around different ethnicities and backgrounds, you hear and see what things certain people go through, and you learn, you experience, why not to do things that are harmful."

If you are selected as a delegate, it is important to include those who haven't gone in your new understanding

The school cafeteria can become a venue for lunchtime events that reach out to the entire school community, such as concerts, poetry readings, or dance demonstrations. Be sure to vary the types of events so many different interests are represented.

of the world and be sure they know that you appreciate what they bring to your life experience.

There are many school climate activities you can engage in to reach out to the entire school community. Here are a few you might want to try:

LUNCHTIME EVENTS

Keeping your student body entertained during the lunch period can be the job of your student government. Many schools have their members partner with one person overseeing all events. Each week, a new team is responsible for lunchtime shows, which might include a friendly competition, a student garage band, an inexpensive giveaway, or student performers in the large gathering areas. This is a chance to get people who may be disconnected from your campus to hook in. Ask them to perform poetry or ask a friend of theirs to sing. People will come out to see their friends. These activities can begin to take on a life of their own as long as it's not the same people over and over again.

RALLIES

An all-school rally can be a fun and unifying activity. You must have a space large enough to fit your entire student body, or you will have to plan two parallel events. People do not like to feel excluded, but some people will not enjoy an assembly no matter what. It is important to keep your assembly full of action and have little "down" time between acts. This is a chance to showcase your season's team captains, flaunt your spirit teams' accomplishments, demonstrate something new, and show school spirit. Be sure you display variety in every assembly held throughout the year. For example, if it's always about the athletes, students will become resentful. Try new things like inviting the African-American Student Union to perform a step dance show or give a brief explanation of the origin of stepping.

DANCES

While most dances are student organized, some schools have been willing to take on the added expense of hiring professional planners to organize dances. A dance is actually quite easy to plan and can be a moneymaker for your school if you share the workload effectively.

One way to share the work is to have every class responsible for one or two dances a year. Once you have a venue for your dance and a D.J. or band, you are halfway there. Most schools use the on campus gym for their dances. Your faculty sponsor can help you book a D.J. Many D.J.s must be booked six to twelve months in advance, so you should always keep an updated list of the top five student choices

Whether you hire a D.J. or a band to play at a school dance, it is important to find one who will set the right tone for the event and keep the atmosphere positive.

for the school's D.J. preference. To do this, you need to evaluate each dance the day you return to school. Your school most likely has a dance and ticket sale policy you should become familiar with. If you are expected to design your own tickets, you will need to vote on a theme at least a month before your scheduled dance so someone can create the ticket for printing. Once you have a theme, you can discuss decorations. You need to have as many people assigned to the clean-up committee as you do to the set-up committee. Remember all of the thoughtful things your custodial staff already does for students and be sure to make their job as easy as possible.

Dances can be fun for your student body and great fundraisers, too. While the faculty has a huge responsibility in supervising and overseeing dances, student responsibility for the event's success is key. A D.J. or band that is able to reflect a climate and atmosphere where students can enjoy themselves and teachers, administrators, and parents can feel good about the event is necessary. The D.J. sets the tone through the music and is the leader of the dance. This person must be someone all parties can trust to set the atmosphere in a positive way. You should hold your D.J. and your students to a high standard as this event is a school-sponsored activity and respect for all is a necessity.

For most dances, students create the theme and do the decorating. Shoddy décor makes people feel as if the dance is not important, while a festive or formal environment will motivate people to behave in a well-mannered way.

CLUBS

The student government, or Associated Student Body (ASB), is responsible for overseeing club activities such as meetings, fundraising, and outings. In order to do this effectively, the ASB must keep communication lines open with the clubs they sponsor. There are many ways of encouraging students to get involved in their school and ASB; one of the best is by offering clubs that appeal to a variety of tastes including service, academic, and other types of clubs. In order to empower students, clubs should be student initiated. At the beginning of each year, all persons who are interested in starting a club or continuing one from the previous year should attend a club orientation workshop. In that workshop, the person responsible for overseeing all clubs and/or ASB funds should explain the procedures to be followed in order for the club to be school sanctioned. As club officers change, it is important that each club petition for membership yearly before being granted permission to utilize the school's name and communication channels. Since clubs are supported by the Associated Student Body, the student government is responsible for encouraging clubs and making sure they follow the necessary protocol. No two clubs with a similar purpose should be allowed.

Students should find peers with similar interests and prepare a club petition that was provided at the orientation meeting. The club petition should show that there are at least ten students on campus who are interested in beginning the club. Obviously, the club objective should be appropriate for school sponsorship. Every club should also have a teacher sponsor, who will be responsible for the direct supervision of the group's activities. By sponsoring a club, teachers are provided with the opportunity to work with students in a non-academic format, which allows them to do what most came into the profession for—to meet and be available for students. These activities help keep a staff vital and plugged into the importance of students learning, through cocurricular activities, the skills students need to develop leadership, teamwork, and communication.

By allowing students the power over their own club and selecting their own sponsor, they begin to build ownership over their club's direction. The sponsor verifies that the direction is school appropriate and club activities can move forward. Sponsors are responsible for supervision, approval of activities, assistance, and guidance. This way, the ASB has both a sponsor and a student government president who they can go to if a problem were to arise. Students need to communicate with their sponsor to obtain approval of their activities and assistance when needed. Students who are original members of the club should solicit additional members by having informational meetings or by sharing information about their club in a way appropriate for your campus, such as a table set up during lunch.

At any school, exclusivity can create a toxic environment, which is why open membership of the entire student body is a must for all school-sponsored clubs. In order to help create a healthy atmosphere, every club on your campus should be open to a wide range of ideas and people. Any club that is unwilling to be open to all members of the student body should be immediately shut down. Students need to learn to work together for their common goals, as that is what is expected in the real

Members of the yearbook club work on page layouts. In many schools, the student government oversees the activities of all school clubs and helps to fund them.

world. High school is the ultimate testing ground for real world experiences.

STUDENT APPRECIATION OF STAFF

Teachers, custodians, support staff, and administrators all like to be reminded of why they choose to work in schools. What better way to reach out to these members of the school community than by thanking them for their efforts? One of the best gifts people working in schools can receive is a note from a student thanking the person for their efforts. These notes can be as simple as, "I saw you picking up trash that my peers left behind and wanted to say thank you for all you do for us when we aren't as thoughtful as we should be," or, "The lesson you taught in English about . . . changed the way I think about . . ." Quick notes of appreciation mean so much to the people who dedicate their lives to working with teens, as results aren't always immediate or visible. Everyone can have a bad day, month or year, but these people come back because they believe in the importance of their product—you. Learning how to communicate with your teachers in a way that is respectful, informational, and engaging is a skill that will gain you incredible respect from peers, teachers, and other adults. A faculty that is supportive of students needs to be given every opportunity to participate in student events. Besides keeping harmony, this builds a stronger community and empathy between students and staff.

FRESHMAN/NEW STUDENT PROGRAMS

Going to a new school can be scary, so adjusting quickly is very important. To reach out to incoming students, the student government can offer tours before school begins and welcome its newcomers with special events. A picnic

Student government can reach out to exchange students to make sure they feel welcome in their new school and have plenty of opportunities to connect with other students.

for the incoming class the day before school starts is a great opportunity for all. If possible, the incoming class can also find their classrooms for the next day. Link Crew, a program sponsored by Learning for Living, Inc., provides a successful model for engaging students socially and academically in your school throughout the year.

Your school can send several students to be trained by the Link Crew with follow-ups throughout the year until your school has established a strong program. If your school doesn't have a program in place for freshmen and transfer students, you should ask your ASB advisor about how to start a Link Crew. You can go to their Web site for more information.

Students who come into a school from another district

Programs such as Link Crew, which train upperclassmen to be school leaders who welcome incoming students, easing their transition to a new school environment, help develop connections between classes on campus.

any time throughout the year should be considered "at-risk" until they have found a group of peers on their new campus. Suicide and dropout rates for transfer students are higher across the country than for other teens. Having a "buddy" program makes the new student and the new student's family feel more at ease. The fear of, "Who will I eat with?" and "Where will I get my food?" is eliminated when a buddy calls the new student to set up a plan for the new student's first day. This can be the beginning of a lifelong relationship or a bridge to making new acquaintances. Either way, it gives a good feeling to all involved.

Exchange students also need to be shown appreciation and made to feel valued on your campus. They bring so much to the culture of a school and are rarely thanked. It is an interesting phenomenon when you find the only students spending social time with exchange students are other exchange students. A buddy program can help here as can student government outreach. It's fine when exchange students connect to one another, but it is important that they have opportunities to connect with American students as well. That's why they signed up for the program. Educating your exchange students about American culture and holidays is something the student government should do constantly. Invite your exchange students to a Thanksgiving feast a week early to show them what to expect, and teach them why it is done. This can be an educational experience for all involved. You can also invite a couple of teachers to thank them for the way they support your international students. A ratio of at least five students for every adult is a good mix.

HOMECOMING/SPIRIT WEEK

Spirit week activities can bring a campus together or be extremely divisive. It is the responsibility of student government to avoid the latter at all costs. There are ways to encourage healthy good-natured competition without resorting to degradation. Yes, each class competes for itself in the spirit wars, but clear rules of engagement must be laid down before spirit competition begins. Members of the student government should agree to a basic set of rules at least one month before spirit week or Homecoming arrives. This gives all classes plenty of time to educate their stakeholders on the rules through homeroom classes, class meetings, or fliers. During this often chaotic time, the president of each class should be sure each class representative is overseeing a portion of the week's events. There should be someone in charge of reporting game information and contestant names to the spirit commissioners, designing

When planning a dance or other special event there are many points to consider, including: location, theme, decorations, music, refreshments, photo opportunities, ticket sales, set-up, and clean-up.

and building a float (if your school is hosting a parade), deciding on appropriate cheers, and leading the class in those cheers. The roles are endless, depending on what is expected at each school site. Obviously, the president can't be in charge of everything, so teamwork is essential.

Classes should follow a theme, as this helps to keep people united. To keep this focused on the whole school, everyone's theme could fall under one umbrella. For example, the school theme might be fairy tales or "Happily Ever After." Each class could take on a specific story. Floats, T-shirts, and other items can be designed by each class to represent the theme while reinforcing the school-wide unity. Other ideas for Homecoming and/or dance themes include:

Western: Think cowboy boots, checkered tablecloths, a

Prom/Homecoming Resources

Trying to plan a prom or Homecoming dance? Check out these online resources for prom/Homecoming committees.

www.hallz.com/prom.htm
A directory of prom venues throughout the United States and Canada, this site allows you to view photographs of many of the facilities.

www.promspot.com
This Web site offers resources for prom and dance committees, including ideas for themes, decorations, and fundraisers, as well as information on the latest prom trends, from dresses to hairstyles and accessories.

www.promnight.com
Offers advice and tips on costs, sites, dinner menus, D.J.s, photographers, and more, as well as ideas for planning Homecoming Week activities.

www.party411.com/prom.html
The site features prom theme ideas and a planning guide, as well as advice on managing prom expenses, selecting favors and invitations, and creating memorable photo opportunities for the attendees.

http://thepromsite.com
Cool ideas for themes, traditions, and parties, as well as checklists, information on budgeting, and more.

www.perfectprom.com
Web site offering tips for prom coordinators and committees, guys, and girls.

www.stumpsspirit.com
A Homecoming and spirit site offering decorations, favors, and ideas and tips for themes, floats, parades, and spirit week activities.

Homecoming week is a great time to plan activities, like all-school rallies, that can show off your school's spirit team and bring your whole campus together to celebrate school spirit and pride.

horseshoe arch, or floats/props consisting of hay bales and fence posts.

Casino: Oversize playing cards, dice, fancy attire, a red and black color scheme, and rented casino tables round out this theme.

Safari: Jungle décor such as vines and trees, and floats or lifesize cutouts featuring wildlife bring this theme to life.

Hawaiian/Luau: Think tiki torches, hula skirts, flower leis, and tropical décor.

Mardi Gras: Masks, feathers, beads, New Orleans inspired décor, or a masquerade ball all complement a Mardi Gras theme.

Patriotic: Red, white, and blue colors provide the focus for this theme, which could also feature U.S.A. icons such as Uncle Sam, or depict events from U.S. history.

Beach Party: Sunglasses, surfboards, beach balls, sand, and beach attire all reinforce the theme.

Medieval/Castles: Floats or props can feature towers,

castles, or fortresses, and cobblestone walkways or stone arches.

Under the Sea: Try nautical props, fish netting, oversize starfish, seahorses, and bubble balloons.

Through the Ages: Each day of Homecoming week could be devoted to a different decade (90s, 80s, 70s, 60s, 50s) with students dressing the part each day. A dance or float from the 50s, for example, could depict a sock hop or a drive-in with boys and girls in 50s dress.

The student government can plan a variety of rallies focused on good-natured competitions in which classes go over the ground rules, compete against one another, and celebrate their goal— winning the Homecoming game. If a class winner is desired, a point system agreed upon by the council members and kept track of by spirit commissioners

Planning a Prom

According to Joe Fontana, Activities Director at Menlo-Atherton High School in Atherton, California, "Planning a May prom begins on the first day of school. If a prom is held outside the school facilities, the contract is usually signed in September. Most of the planning should be done in the first few weeks.

"Deciding on a theme, ticket prices, and printing, lining up chaperones, securing a D.J. or band and photographer, decorating a photo background, designating who on your committee will be responsible for what tasks—the sooner all these things are done, the easier it will be when the crunch of the last month's chores hit you. Setting up a timeline and ticket selling procedures are essential.

"Some schools reinvent the process every year. Others maintain a manual that's added to or improved with each year's experience, providing a template for each new committee."

and/or an adult can be used. Classes should have cheers they can chant as a group at these rallies. These cheers should be in good taste and approved by the class's teacher advisor.

Breakfast rallies can also be a lot of fun as well as a fundraising opportunity to offset the expense of the week. Everyone can come to school early one day and meet in the gym for breakfast. Classes can stand together in the four corners of the room yelling their cheers the loudest and eating donuts and milk.

Another way to bring your classes together can be the last time students are allowed to work on their floats. If the structure of the float is created off campus, the skeleton can be brought onto campus and placed in a secure location such as an auto shop or a custodial shed until the night before display. On the last evening of float work, students should be encouraged to stay on campus from the time school releases until the float is complete. Parents are usually open to donating a dinner which students can then purchase at a nominal price, offsetting the cost of the float materials.

As you can see, Homecoming Week requires thorough planning, inclusive activities, and a variety of students from all corners of campus.

All of the activities and events mentioned in this chapter require thorough planning. It is important that student government members allow ample time for the planning and scheduling of any events they want to hold. Most schools plan their schedules in April and May for the following year. It is best that you communicate your desires early. When there are many groups of people who need to be informed of or help with a plan, you will need time to work with your school's stakeholders (anyone who is invested in your school: students, teachers, administrators, parents, community members). Also, many prom and Homecoming venues book early. Proms are often in competition with company parties and weddings that can pay more, so you may need to get a contract early.

After you have a project date, think of your project in six stages. First, set a goal. What is the purpose of your event? Look over notes of those who have completed similar events. How will you structure the event to meet your goal? Next, plan out, step by step, what will occur. Run this by two friends and your advisor before taking it to the larger group so they can help you look for possible holes you haven't filled in yet. When you're ready, present your idea to your student council. Be very prepared when you do this; there's nothing worse than feeling put on the spot because you haven't planned well. Once the plan has been approved, complete the steps you laid out for yourself or oversee those who are assisting you in the fulfillment of your goal. Never ask anyone to do something you are not willing to do yourself or you will lose respect from those you need support from the most. Now follow through and enjoy the fruits of your labor. You've done an army's work; enjoy it.

Finally, all good planning of student government activities should be followed up with an evaluation of what went well and what can be improved upon for the next time. No job is done until the evaluation is complete. The outline of each event, including who was responsible for what, and the event evaluation, should be kept in a binder for next year's leaders to refer to. ASB binders provide a record of how much you've accomplished and they make a great guide for the future.

Pitch a ball, hit the target, and burst a water balloon over someone's head. Renting a booth like this for a school carnival or fair is one way to raise funds for your school.

3

Fundraising

Fundraising is necessary for most student governments so that they can raise the money needed to carry out school activities and events.

Many schools sell cards that offer students discounts at various school-sponsored activities such as dances, plays, athletic events, and concerts. Annual sales of these cards can form the basis for your student government's budget. You can work with different departments to be sure there is an incentive for students to purchase a card. The money generated by card sales goes to support school-sponsored activities as well as your school climate events.

Raising money is most effective when it is an integral part of your campus activities, not a specific plea for funding. Charging a few dollars more for dances, school-wide breakfasts, dinners, plays, concerts, and athletic events are other ways to provide adequate funding.

Registering your campus for eScrip is another easy way to gather funds. eScrip is a program with which families

Fundraising Ideas for Your School

State associations of student councils offer conferences, camps, workshops, and scholarships, and many of their Web sites contain useful ideas and information. For example, Oregon's State Student Council Association Web site, **<www.oasc.org>**, has a full section for sharing fundraising ideas.

Here's a sample:

- Sell pizza from a local pizza restaurant at basketball and football games. We have them cut it into eight slices and sell them for two dollars each. Just be careful who you have sell the pizzas because we once had one person eat about half a pizza while selling it.

- Sell donuts at morning break.

- Hold a sock hop. Invite the surrounding schools or allow students to bring up to three guests.

- Hold a carnation or rose drive. Carnations can be dyed to match school colors. At Homecoming and Valentine's Day we sell flowers and you put a note with it. This gets a lot of money and we have fun doing it.

- Hold a kiss the pig contest, where there are jars with certain names on them. Students donate money to the person's jar that they want to see kiss the pig.

- Two rival schools make lists of eight people in the other school that they would like to see get a pie in the face. The school that raises the most money in a given time gets to pie the faces of the people on their list.

- The week of Valentine's Day, sell cans of Crush soda for a dollar. People buy them and have them sent to their crushes. For another dollar they can buy insurance to block their name, so the person who received it doesn't know who sent it. The person receiving it can pay a dollar to find out if the sender has insurance or not.

can register their credit cards so your school receives a percentage of all purchases made using the registered card. See your school's auditor to get the account number for your families to register and begin earning funds for your budget. The less time you spend on fundraising, the more time you can spend having fun.

According to efundraising.com, the following are essential to a successful fundraiser:

- A clear goal stating how much money needs to be raised and how the funds will be spent.
- An organized, enthusiastic, and available leader.
- A timespan for the fundraiser (anywhere from a few days to a few weeks).

Every student body has a budget from which they work. Your student government will vote on a tentative budget in the spring and finalize that budget in the fall after the monies have been collected for student body cards and other items. In some cases these monies may include income from annual fundraisers such as the sale of academic planners, or other fundraisers your school has built in. In Palo Alto, California, one of these moneymaking endeavors is built around the locale of the school. One of the city's two public high schools is located right across the street from the Stanford University football stadium. Selling parking during Stanford's home football games can bring in large amounts of money and the two high schools work together to earn and split the proceeds. This takes a lot of time, people, and support, but it is worth the trouble.

Think about what unique opportunities your community has that might allow your school to earn money while performing a community service. Maybe there is a local festival you can sell parking spaces for. Or you could host a food concession or other booth at a county fair. Consider

Student governments can raise money by selling promotional items at their school store, such as sweatshirts, T-shirts, and more.

starting a city fair as many schools have done. Open a school store, where you can sell items with your school's logo imprinted on them, such as T-shirts, sweatshirts, mugs, notebooks, baseball caps, and pens and pencils. Bake sales and car washes are reliable fundraisers. Another fundraising idea is to offer to wrap Christmas presents for teachers or do personal shopping for a small donation. They might be grateful to you for relieving them of the time and pressure needed to search out a particular item for a young child or teenager.

You can also try asking some of your better-known teachers to spend fifteen minutes in a dunk tank. Auction off the first pitch to the highest bidder, then charge a few dollars a pitch. Students on campus can make the dunk tanks or they can be rented.

At Gunn High School in Palo Alto, California, students developed a pie-your-teacher fundraiser. Although some teachers felt this kind of fundraiser was inappropriate, others did not mind participating. Students paid $1 each

Participants in The Leaders Forum Core Camp brainstorm ways to make the new school year unique through activities and events that bring the whole campus together.

for a whipped cream pie, which they could throw at the participating teachers, who were dressed in trash bags and goggles. The fundraiser was a huge success.

If further fundraising is needed, there are numerous organizations that are willing to help you raise funds by selling things like candy, cookie dough, magazines, scratch cards, flower bulbs, wrapping paper, or candles, but check out these organizations with your advisor and the Better Business Bureau. If the fundraising company you're considering working with won't give you back at least 40 percent, you may not want to work with them. All revenue options should be assessed by your student government and campus administration.

If your school does not have a full-time bookkeeper to help the student government keep track of finances, consider using software programs that can keep you up to

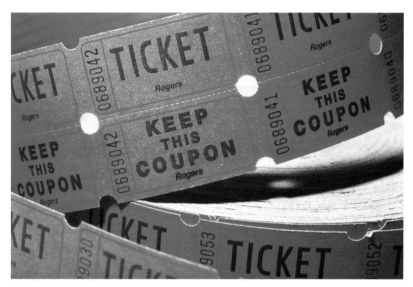

Holding a raffle is one way to raise funds for the student council or government. Ask local retailers if they might be willing to donate products free or at cost.

date on income and expenditures. Often your school's bookkeeper must wait for the district office to release the monthly statement. That won't be done until the district is in balance with your county office. Having your own bookkeeper and software benefits your whole school. The student government, guidance, library, and testing departments will all benefit, so encourage them to help finance the purchase of software. Blue Bear Software has excellent programs they can tailor to meet your school's needs, giving your student government access to spreadsheets that tell you how many tickets you sold to the dance, who purchased them, and what your total income and expenses were. It also helps you keep track of your school store's finances and inventory.

This way you know if you can have more balloons at the dance or if you need to cut back on your expenses at a moment's notice.

Remember, the goal of your fundraising is to earn the money necessary to enjoy a rewarding school year full of fun activities and events for the entire student body, so be sure to keep everyone motivated and working toward this common goal.

Leadership takes many forms. Making new members of your school community feel welcome, helping them find their classes, or sitting with them at lunch, are all ways you can show leadership at your school.

4

Leadership Beyond Government

There are many opportunities for leadership beyond student government. If you are a student leader, you may want to become involved in your school's anti-drug program, peer mentoring program, conflict resolution program, or student court. Or you may want to take your leadership skills out into the community and get involved in a school-sponsored service project or attend a national leadership conference so you can share ideas with other student leaders.

ANTI-DRINKING/DRUG LEADERSHIP

Stress—tension, worry, doubt, anger—is part of life. Everybody encounters people and situations that are unpleasant and stressful. Parents may say or do something you don't understand or agree with. They may make rules you consider unfair, or load expectations onto you that you don't think you can meet. Teachers, friends—real or phony—may say or do things that upset you.

Reacting to all these things with anger is normal. Growing up isn't easy; that's what the expression "growing pains" means.

The difference in how stress affects people lies in how they deal with it. What students do with this stress is as much the responsibility of the student government as the parents, teachers, and administrators. Planning stress releasers at lunch and after school can help. But there may be times when you need to teach your peers yourself. What are students doing with their stress? Are they dancing, playing music, taking bubble baths, crying, talking to trusted friends, doing mindful breathing exercises, drinking, using drugs? Obviously, some of these options are healthier than others. Stress exists; how one manages stress is the real test.

If you were to ask a teenager at a high school if they use alcohol or other drugs, chances are, they'd say "No." That's

Famous Faces in Student Government

Many successful people began to acquire leadership skills by being active in student government, including:

- Malcolm X, African-American leader and activist

- Donald Trump, entrepreneur

- Richard Nixon, United States President

- Janet Reno, U.S. Attorney General for the Clinton administration

- John Ashcroft, U.S. Attorney General for the George W. Bush administration

- Rosie O'Donnell, actress and activist

- Kevin Spacey, actor

what they're supposed to say, right? If you were to ask the same student if there is an alcohol/drug problem on their campus, you'd probably get a resounding "Yes."

It is an interesting occurrence that while most students claim they do not use controlled substances, they often claim that everyone else does. This perception was once so prevalent on college campuses that many students drank more than they desired in an attempt to "keep up" with their peers, whom they assumed were drinking more than they were. This frightening trend drove many colleges to educate their students through media campaigns on social norms. This idea has since made its way into middle and high schools. Educators have long known that the idea of "everyone's doing it" is wrong thinking. Using a scientific survey to find out exactly what everyone is doing in a no-threat environment gives student leaders a chance to combat perception with reality. The purpose of this exercise is to inform students about the actual drinking or drug habits of their peers through clear and consistent messages so that their behavior is based on fact and not inaccurate perceptions. The overall goal of a social norms media campaign is to reduce the incidence of alcohol or drug-related negative consequences on campus. If there are concerns about the level of use on your campus, then a social norms media campaign is a great project to look into.

The Most of Us project in Bozeman, Montana, is on the cutting edge of working with high schools using a social normative approach. This is education in one of its purest forms. Students take an on-line survey created by professionals. Once results are received, usually within a week, students can run a media campaign to inform their peers of what the school's typical beliefs are regarding drugs, alcohol, seat belt use, and other risky behaviors. The school

Student leaders look for ways to get involved in their community, both inside and outside of school. Service projects, such as fall cleanups for elderly homeowners, are a great way for students to make a positive impact on the local community.

art department can be involved in the design of posters with images or graphics that appeal to your population. Your engineering/computer students can design screen savers that show the factoids on computers across campus. The possibilities for education and marketing can come alive right in your own school.

PEER COUNSELING/CONFLICT RESOLUTION

In addition to traditional student government, some schools have a peer counseling/conflict resolution program. Many of the negative encounters that students experience in high school are based on miscommunication. Talking the problem out with an unbiased third party in a confidential setting can clear the air between students before the problem balloons into an issue the school's administration must deal with as a discipline problem.

Peer counseling or "peer helping" training offers students alternatives to violence and teaches them conflict resolution strategies such as one-on-one student counseling, individual and group peer education, and peer conflict mediation.

Peer education may involve classroom presentations made by student leaders covering topics like racism, diversity, gangs, and gay/lesbian issues. In some schools peer education is a standard part of the curriculum. The National Youth Violence Prevention Resource Center is an excellent resource for students interested in becoming involved in conflict resolution or peer helping.

Conflict resolution training programs generally teach student leaders how to establish ground rules between disputing parties, gather perspectives from each person by listening without interruption, find common interests among the disputing parties, create options or possible solutions to the problem, evaluate these options, and create an agreement.

STUDENT COURT

Student courts can be set up for students to bring their administrative and discipline issues before their peers to be adjudicated. This kind of court may be illegal in your state. Your administration can check the legality in your state if this is something you'd like to implement. Students could be referred to student court for a variety of misdeeds including attendance, fighting, or theft. A court comprising fellow student body members would hear the arguments from each side and determine innocence or guilt. If guilt is found, the student court could impose a punishment appropriate to the indiscretion. It depends on your state and your school's comfort with such a system, but this can

Prudential Spirit of Community Awards

The Prudential Spirit of Community Awards go to student leaders in grades five through twelve who demonstrate exemplary community service. Sponsored by Prudential Financial and the National Association of Secondary School Principals (NASSP), this program offers nominees $1,000 in cash and an all-expenses-paid trip to Washington D.C. in May, when the top ten national honorees each receive $5,000, a gold medallion, and a crystal trophy for their school. For more information visit: **<www.principals.org/awards/prudential.cfm>**. Here is a list of the 2004 national winners and their prize-winning projects:

- **Whitney Buesgens,** 17, of Slayton, Minnesota, founded the first independent overnight "grief camp" in the upper Midwest for children who have lost a loved one.

- **Elyse Monti,** 17, of East Greenwich, Rhode Island, founded a statewide support group for teens with obsessive-compulsive disorder (OCD), raised $17,000 for research into OCD, and chaired a national Obsessive Compulsive Youth Advisory Board.

- **Samuel Nassie,** 16, of Paradise, California, located, recorded, and mapped the gravesites of nearly two thousand military veterans buried in his community's cemeteries so they would not be forgotten. Samuel said, "It was extremely important to me to make sure that the veterans of my community be recognized and remembered with the respect that they have earned by serving our nation so selflessly."

- **Meghan Pasricha,** 18, of Hockessin, Delaware, started a worldwide campaign to educate young people about the hazards of tobacco use. She later presented her project at the World Health Organization's Conference on Tobacco in Finland.

- **Erin Rosen-Watson,** 17, of Natick, Massachusetts, formed a non-profit corporation called "Erin's Helping Hands" to carry out projects to help needy children in her state.

- **Amanda Crowe,** 13, of Upton, Massachusetts, coordinated book-collecting drives for six years to supply reading material to hospital waiting rooms, shelters, and literacy programs. Her spring and fall book collections yield more than 10,000 books a year. According to Amanda, "So many kids take it for granted that they have good books and know how to read. By working on this project, volunteers see how lucky they are to be in a safe house, able to read, and not sick like the children in the hospital."

- **Alexandra Holdeman,** 10, of Mishawaka, Indiana, collected more than twelve hundred bundles of baby clothing, blankets, diapers, and other supplies for infants born to single and teenaged mothers.

- **Jenessa Largent,** 12, of White Bear Lake, Minnesota, designed and distributed sixty thousand "freedom bracelets" for U.S. soldiers serving overseas and their families. Jenessa solicited donations of the supplies needed and recruited students at her school to help make the bracelets. On her Web site she asked for donations to defray the costs of postage.

- **Warner Phipps,** 15, of Kearny, Nebraska, designed and taught grain bin safety workshops throughout his state. After a local student died in a grain bin accident, he learned that grain bin entrapment is a leading cause of injury or death on farms. With help from his family, his county 4-H leader, and volunteers from the local FFA organization, Warner has delivered his message in safety presentations to over 73,000 people.

- **Anna Rose,** 13, of Elizabeth, Colorado, created "Sight Angels," a non-profit organization that has provided more than five thousand pairs of eyeglasses and other ocular supplies to homeless shelters, clinics, and needy individuals. Anna let potential eyewear donors know about her project, created a Web site, and solicited funds to purchase supplies. Since then, Sight Angels has become the primary reading glasses supplier to the Denver Rescue Mission, the Colorado Coalition for the Homeless, and the Stout Street Clinic.

be an effective way of keeping an open and fair climate in your school if the people involved are serious about the responsibility before them.

LEADERSHIP TRAINING

There are numerous resources for student leadership opportunities both in your school and community. Nationwide, there is the National Association of Student Councils (NASC), which alternates its conventions between the east and west every summer. In California, the California Association of Student Leaders (CASL) is a major student leadership organization. They hold their state convention for middle and high schools in March each year. Separate leadership training sessions for middle and high schools are held during the summer. The conference

NASC Difference Makers Awards

In addition to the satisfaction that comes from being of service to others, there are many tangible awards presented annually in regional and national programs to recognize outstanding accomplishments in the community. The National Association of Student Councils (NASC) sponsors Difference Makers Awards as part of its National Student Leadership Week in April of each year. Winners in 2004 included:

- Monroe County High School, Monroeville, Alabama, for its "Operation Baghdad" project.

- Wagar Middle School, Carleton, Michigan, for its "Valentines for Veterans and Active Servicemen" project.

- Pine Hill Middle School, Pine Hill, New Jersey, for its "Holiday Food Drive."

- Fairport High School, Fairport, New York, for its "Brotherhood-Sisterhood Week."

teaches students new ways to get involved in their school and encourage others to be involved. While this conference is unique, there are similar ones in many places around the United States.

For help with selecting a leadership conference, ask the person in charge of your student government. There are many leadership conferences available, but be cautious of any conference that charges a lot of money and does not offer scholarships. Some conferences are run strictly for profit, and though they may be good ones, look closely at what you are getting in return. Find out who runs the conference you are interested in and how they are connected to schools. Some businesses running leadership camps send out random mailings. They may have no ties to any schools or school-affiliated organization. Your student government advisor can help you identify a conference that is worthwhile for you and will best help you establish the skills you are seeking to develop. Most reputable organizations will allow you to apply on-line, but call first to make sure you get all the information you need to determine if this conference is the right one for you.

TAKING LEADERSHIP INTO THE COMMUNITY

You hear a lot about self-esteem: How good do you feel about yourself? How worthy do you feel? How much respect do you think you deserve? To be comfortable, happy, even proud of the kind of person you are is what self-esteem is all about.

Some books talk about how getting good grades or making a team can cause you to feel good about yourself. There's another way to earn the respect of others and add to your self-esteem: doing something for somebody else, making a difference in someone's life. Esteem means value;

becoming a person of value to others leads to a feeling of personal value.

Leadership in community service can mean joining a student service group, initiating a group project, or volunteering on an individual basis. Your student council might adopt a group project. Some state student council associations adopt statewide charities and projects. Nebraska's official charity is the Make-A-Wish Foundation, for which Bennington High School raised $1,500 in 2003–2004. The state's student council project called for student council members to read to elementary children on a regular basis, maybe thirty minutes once or twice a week or month. The association's goal was thirty thousand books to be read during the year.

But even if you aren't a member of the student council, you can do something similar on your own. Individual service projects don't require a lot of organization, just some initiative. Initiative is a form of leadership, even if you're doing something alone. Perhaps you know of an elderly or disabled person who could use some help with simple chores around the house: shopping, cleaning, yardwork, cooking. If you don't know of any, there is an agency where you live who can find them for you.

If you're looking for ideas on how to be of service, a good place to start is at the Web site of Youth Service America (YSA). National projects, such as the Great American Bake Sale to help end child hunger in America, depend on individuals like you doing their part in their own home towns.

Millions of young Americans participate in the annual National Youth Service Day in mid-April. You might tutor or read to a child, register voters, collect recyclable material, or distribute health and nutrition information. There are many ways to demonstrate your leadership in your community, either on your own or as an active member of a student organization.

YSA also sponsors a Global Youth Service Day in April each year, when young people in more than one hundred countries carry out service projects to improve the lives of their neighbors, and, in so doing, improve their own lives as well.

Ralph Waldo Emerson summed up the value of leadership in community service in a poem which reads, in part:

> To leave the world a bit better,
>
> whether by a healthy child,
>
> a garden patch, or a redeemed social condition,
>
> to know even one life has breathed easier
>
> because you have lived.
>
> This is to have succeeded.

For many students, the most important things they remember about their school years are the things they did outside the classroom. Getting involved in leadership activities, whether planning a dance or a week of Homecoming activities, mentoring a fellow student, or performing community service, will teach you new skills and leave you with lasting memories of your school days.

Glossary

associated student body (ASB)–another term for the student government.

civic–pertaining to citizenship and the concerns of the community.

cocurricular–school-related activities that take place outside the classroom.

constitution–a statement of the fundamental principles by which a group is to be governed.

due process–fairness, as in giving a person a chance to be heard in a disciplinary action.

leadership–the ability to motivate people to get things done and fulfill a mission.

peer–a person of the same rank or standing.

privileges–activities in which participation must be earned and can be denied; not guaranteed by law.

rights–activities where participation is guaranteed by law and may be denied only with due process.

student council–a group of elected or appointed students responsible for planning and carrying out many cocurricular activities.

Internet Resources

www.charactercounts.org
A nonprofit organization that offers discussions on topics relating to its six pillars of character: trustworthiness, respect, responsibility, fairness, caring, and citizenship.

www.linkcrew.com
The Link Crew Program trains upperclassmen to be leaders who can help ease the transition to high school for incoming freshmen.

www.theleadersforum.com
A private leadership company offering camps for high school and middle school students.

www.nasc.us
The National Association of Student Councils Web site.

www.nassp.org
The National Association of Secondary School Principals Web site provides information on conventions, awards programs, and online articles from its *Leadership Magazine*.

www.safeyouth.org
The Web site of the National Youth Violence Prevention Center offers information on conflict resolution and peer helping programs.

www.servenet.org
The Web site of Youth Service America.

Further Reading

Canfield, Jack L. *Chicken Soup for the Teenage Soul.* Edison, New Jersey: Health Communications Inc., 1997.

Carnegie, Dale. *The Leader in You.* New York: Pocket Books, 1995.

Covey, Sean. *7 Habits of Highly Effective Teens.* New York: Simon & Schuster, 2003.

Covey, Stephen R. *7 Habits of Highly Effective People.* Philadelphia: Running Press Book Publishers, 1998.

Jacobs, Thomas A. *What Are My Rights?* Minneapolis: Free Spirit Publishing Inc., 1997.

Lewis, Barbara A. *The Kid's Guide to Social Action.* Minneapolis: Free Spirit Publishing Inc., 1998.

Lewis, Barbara A. *What Do You Stand For?* Minneapolis: Free Spirit Publishing Inc., 1997.

Maxwell, John C. *The 21 Indispensable Qualities of a Leader: Becoming the Person Others Will Want to Follow.* Nashville: Nelson Books, 1999.

West, Edie. *Big Book of Ice Breakers.* Columbus, Ohio: McGraw-Hill, 1997.

Index

PICTURE CREDITS

ABOUT THE AUTHOR

Joann Vaars is a teacher on special assignment at Palo Alto High School. Having taught special education and English, she became passionate about working with teenagers on their social and emotional development. She took the position of Director of Student Activities and has since become a member of the California Activities Directors Association. She lives in Menlo Park, California, with her husband, son, grandmother, and cat. Currently, she is working towards a second Master's degree and a Tier 1 Administrative Credential.

SERIES CONSULTANT

Series Consultant Sharon L. Ransom is Chief Officer of the Office of Standards-Based Instruction for Chicago Public Schools and Lecturer at the University of Illinois at Chicago. She is the founding director of the Achieving High Standards Project: a Standards-Based Comprehensive School Reform project at the University of Illinois at Chicago, and she is the former director of the Partnership READ Project: a Standards Based Change Process. Her work has included school reform issues that center on literacy instruction, as well as developing standards-based curriculum and assessments, improving school leadership, and promoting school, parent, and community partnerships. In 1999, she received the Martin Luther King Outstanding Educator's Award.